MARTHA, REALLY AND CRUELLY

MW01107066

OTHER BOOKS BY TOM CONNOR AND JIM DOWNEY

Is Martha Stuart Living?
Martha Stuart's Better Than You at Entertaining
Martha Stuart's Excrutiatingly Perfect Weddings
Re-Wired
Smyth & Hawk'em Gardening Catalog
Zeguts: Ridiculous Restaurants

MARTHA, REALLY AND CRUELLY

The Completely Unauthorized Autobiography

Tom Connor and Jim Downey

Andrews McMeel
Publishing

Kansas City

Martha, Really and Cruelly

Copyright © 2003 by Tom Connor and Jim Downey. All rights reserved.
Printed in the United States of America. No part of this book may be used or
reproduced in any manner whatsoever without written permission except in the
case of reprints in the context of reviews. For information, write Andrews
McMeel Publishing, an Andrews McMeel Universal company, 4520 Main Street,
Kansas City, Missouri 64111.

03 04 05 06 07 RR2 10 9 8 7 6 5 4 3 2 1

Library of Congress Cataloging-in-Publication Data

Connor, Tom.
  Martha, really and cruelly : my true life story / Tom Connor and Jim Downey.
      p. cm.
    ISBN: 0-7407-3320-6
      1. Stewart, Martha—Parodies, imitations, etc. 2. American wit and humor. I.
Downey, Jim. II. Title.

PN6231.P3C657 2003
818'.5407—dc21

2003043691

Attention: Schools and Businesses

Andrews McMeel books are available at quantity discounts with bulk purchase
for educational, business, or sales promotional use. For information, please write
to: Special Sales Department, Andrews McMeel Publishing, 4520 Main Street,
Kansas City, Missouri 64111.

This book is dedicated to the
one person on the planet who is capable of
completeing all of my home projects.
Guess who.

CONTENTS

Contents

Contents

Acknowledgments

I acknowledge the right to bear glue guns, the limited powers of the Securities Exchange Commission, my innocence, and the absolute moral authority of the Roman Catholic hierarchy, without which the faithful would be screwed.

Introduction

Autobiographies are perfect opportunities to clean house. Not to impress or deceive—not to gild the lily, polish the image, embroider the truth, stencil the bidet—but to throw out the myths and reveal a person's life as it has really been lived.

Many people assume, for example, that I achieved success only later in life, but this simply isn't true. I've been phenomenally successful my entire life, beginning with my first business when I was ten.

Martha's Original Bug Juice stand was an immediate hit. (Actually, to be perfectly honest, this was my second entrepreneurial venture. The first, Martha's Original Kool-Aid® Stand, operated in the same location on the sidewalk in front of my parents' house in Nutley, New Jersey. However, it was forced out of business after attorneys for Kool-Aid® served me with a cease-and-desist order for trademark infringement. The case is still in litigation.) Mine was also the very first juice stand to be equipped with a customer service line in the form of tins cans strung between the stand and my public relations manager and best friend's house next door.

At any rate, even then I knew that I had to use the best and most authentic ingredients I could find. Unfortunately, what people failed to appreciate at the time was that bugs are not only delicious but they are an important source of protein for children in many countries of the world. I can now reveal for the first time that my secret recipe called for ladybugs, yellow jackets, and praying mantises. When mixed with lincolnberries for coloring (I think they were lincolnberries; see "A Birthday Party Turns Ugly"), rubbing alcohol for liquidity, and a soupçon more or less of codeine for taste. The result proved irresistible not only to kids on the block but kids from other neighborhoods and teenagers from surrounding towns.

In fact, Martha's Original Bug Juice was so successful that a year after opening I received an offer for the business from Bunny Baker, a dweeby but ambitious boy who lived up the street. Ready for something more challenging, I agreed to sell on condition that the deal close quickly.

I mention that clause in the contract because it

became a key point in court. At issue was the timing
of the sale. How early, Bunny's attorney wanted to
know, was I aware of customer complaints to the local
health department? At what point did I learn that the
stand was under FDA as well as Alcohol, Tobacco, and
Firearms investigations? And why, on the afternoon of
Friday, June 19, did I insist that Mr. Baker hand over
his piggy bank and tooth-fairy money minutes before
investigators rolled up to the curb to close the stand
down?

On the stand, Bunny claimed I'd received a tip
that morning from my friend Joan, whose mother
worked for the health department. I remembered no
such conversation (the tin can was jumping with calls
that particular day), nor was there any record of the
call, of course, so it was my word against his and
Joan's, who also testified against me. (Bunny, or
William R. Baker III, as he prefers being called these
days, would eventually gain a small measure of success
as associate director of enforcement at the Securities
and Exchange Commission. Joan is currently in the
government's witness protection program and
believed to be living in Indiana, in a city like Terra
Haute, at, say, 1219 South Street, Apt. 3A)

Yet there was no real need for a trial. I was tried in
the local media (the *Nutley Weekly Shopper & Coupon
Saver* was particularly savage in its coverage) long
before the case was heard. In the end, I returned
Bunny's money and agreed to refrain from doing
business in the beverage industry for twenty years. But
that isn't the point. The point is that people hate
those who are more creative, intelligent, talented, and
successful than they are, and will do anything they can
to punish us for our superiority.

This has been the story of my life. Now the whole
world will know what it's like to be Martha, really and
cruelly.

ANCESTORS

*M*ost people are surprised to learn that I'm not a native New England WASP (though probably not as surprised as I was when I found out). Actually, I'm descended from two lines of Old World peoples who were among the earliest and most primitive settlers of what is now northern Poland.

The Koskos, my father's clan, were a fearsome clan of vole hunters from the village of Lebork. In addition to controlling the vole-pelt trade in that part of the known world, Lebork villagers were famous for retaining their personal solid waste and utilizing it in everything from cooking fuel and yurt construction materials to ammo and joke doo-doo pads.

My mother's people, the Dumbrowskis, were short, secretive, shrub-dwellers from the nearby village of Slupsk (which, in Polish, means either "they who would have you think otherwise of them" or "you have no evidence of that.") Slupskies, at the time, possessed the only known written directions on how to drink from a cup.

According to legend, Leborkers and Slupskies loathed one another 364 days out of the year. But on February 13, which of course is the Feast of St. Stanislaus the Licentious, Lebork men would slip into Slupsk at noon and be carried off by the most desirable female Slupskies for their wives. (I'm told I was named for a great Slupsk beauty—my mother's great-aunt, Martha the Often Leborked.)

Now in those days, women were prized not for their faces or figures but for three more substantive qualities: the amount of hair on their bodies, especially the underarms, which they wore tightly braided and coiled; their way with a kielbasa; and their ability to carry their men home after a night of drinking and carousing in the goat yards.

Which is how my mother won my father. The following spring, in 1939, a tightening of the public bathing laws forced the evacuation of both villages, and the newlyweds left Poland for New Jersey, the state most resembling, culturally and spiritually, their homeland.

Thus began the next chapter in the long and glorious history of the Koskos in America. And what an amazing chapter it would turn out to be, as you'll soon discover.

INFANCY

*T*he delivery-room ceiling was eggshell white. Instantly, I knew I'd arrived in the right place. Life looked perfect as long as I gazed upward, but the moment I turned upside down, things got ugly.

Hoisted high by my ankles, I let out a wail—not for the sharp slap on my buttocks, which I vividly remember enjoying, but from the view. Below me, past dozens of bassinets filled with blue and pink bundles, I saw that the hospital walls were painted a canned LeSeur pea–green and the floor laid in yellow-speckled, crabgrass-green linoleum. These were hardly the colors I would have chosen for my entrance into existence.

Yet as miserable as I was, in those first few minutes I glimpsed my destiny. No, not to redecorate hospitals—I was on Earth to control my environment, and everyone else's! I had no words for this at the time, of course, but from day one I knew that in time I would design and manufacture my own line of paints. And once I controlled color, I knew the other elements of the universe would quickly fall in step.

A BIRTHDAY PARTY TURNS UGLY

*M*y first catering job was my sister Laura's seventh birthday party. She now says she never wanted me to bake and serve—she claims she didn't even want me *invited* to the party! That Laura, what a jokester!

Nevertheless, I began preparations a month before the big day by going over the guest list with my mother. After inviting myself and a handful of adults I'd identified as potential clients, I spent weeks carefully considering a suitable recipe. Rather than serve something childish, like an ice-cream cake, or mindlessly entertaining, like a chocolate layer cake, I sought a dessert that would be as nutritious as it was delicious while making a statement; I wanted to be remembered long after the strains of "and belong in a zoo" had drifted above the backyard, neighborhood, and town, off into space.

In the end I decided to go with a lincolnberry multilayered torte (at least I think they were lincolnberries) with whipped apricot filling and a Brussels sprout demiglaze.

It still hurts that Laura blamed what happened that day on my baking. Of course, large chunks of undigested cake *were* found spewed all over the backyard. In addition to what can only be termed mass hysteria and violent projectile vomiting, many of the guests (including not a few of the adults, I might add) threw whole wedges of birthday cake at me.

For weeks afterward they complained of severe stomach cramps and hallucinations, but did anyone consider how *I* felt? In what would prove to be the story of my childhood, no one understood at the time what I was trying to achieve. While everyone was making a fuss over Laura—"Oh it's her *birth*day, oh let's have a *party*, oh let's give her *presents*!"—I was just trying to get a little something for *me*. A little recognition, a little respect.

Yet as I told the emergency medical technicians who arrived at the scene, this was never about birthdays or cake or attention. It was about the courage to test new recipes. It was about the gifts of food and sisterhood. It was about the start of a career, the start of a real life, the start of a freaking *legend*, goddamnit! Worst of all, to this day Laura still hasn't paid my invoice for the party!

Another girl would have thrown the oven mitt in after an incident like this, but not me. I chalked the party up to experience and walked away from it with a steelier resolve and a valuable lesson: When offering to perform a service for family or friends, never leave a paper trail of recipes or messages, and always get paid up front!

NUTLEY

I grew up in the small, working-class town of Nutley, New Jersey. Actually, it had been settled in the Colonial era as the town of Wellesley but was renamed in the early 1940s, shortly after my family moved in.

Our home was an old white farmhouse at the end of Hidden Drive—a crazy-quilt neighborhood of first- and second-generation Eastern European families, many of whom were related to us in one way or another.

Dad's brother Uncle Leudi and Mom's sister Aunt Judi lived with their children in a small house a block away on Slow Children Lane. I spent a lot of time at their house playing Hide the Kielbasa with cousins Rudi and Hooti and watching little Petuti eat mud, which she would scoop out of the flower beds with both hands, as if eating from a trough of homemade fudge. Behind us, on Falling Rocks Road, lived Grandpops Dumbrowksi, my maternal grandfather and a World War I veteran who'd been mustard-gassed at Ypres. Twice a year, he would parade down the middle of the street, naked save for a helmet, rubbing baked ham all over his body and shouting "Excelsior!" I always meant to ask him what kind of mustard the enemy used.

Two streets away, on Dangerous Curve Highway, lived still other relatives, Cousins Helen and George Metsky, and next door to them my best friend, Trudi Tricksa.

No one had TV in those days, much less computers or cell phones, yet I never recall being bored. For one thing, Dad would bring home free samples from his job as a pharmaceutical salesman, which we passed around the neighborhood. For another, there was simply too much to do outdoors!

I strung daisy chains around our house and yard in the spring, constructed snow replicas of the Kremlin in the winter, and on hot summer days cooked Western omelettes on the sidewalks for the neighborhood boys. (Recently, I came across my original recipe for this treat, handwritten on a three-by-five index card and copyrighted © 1957: "First, prepare the cooking surface by washing a foot-square area of concrete with one part hydrogen peroxide to three parts vodka, allowing to dry in the sun. Then brush generously with any good, lightweight oil, new or recycled, it doesn't matter, and sprinkle with dandelion pollen before pouring on eggs—three robins' eggs or eight sparrows'—cheese or lumpy milk clots, and pieces of ham or diced pink Spaldeen rubber balls. Improvisation is the key ingredient!") After an al fresco meal like this, I would pass around after-brunch cattails for the boys to smoke, followed by small cups of strong, dark creek water.

Things changed when I went away to college. At the age of fifteen, Trudi murdered every member of her family, including the pet sloths. Uncle Leudi left Aunt Judi for Trudi, marrying her one visiting day in 1953 and moving to a trailer court half a mile from the state prison for the criminally insane. Cousin George Metsky was arrested as the Mad Bomber. And

Grandpops Dumbrowski was named Grand Marshall
of the Memorial Day parade at Bellevue Hospital.

Still, some of the happiest times of my life
occurred in that screwy little town. Although I'm
global now, with homes in many of the most exclusive
towns and cities in the world, I sometimes go back to
Nutley in my mind, just walking through the old
neighborhood, peering in windows, entering through
unlocked doors or open windows, rearranging
furniture and collecting dustballs for my collection
(see my chapter "Collecting").

I guess a part of me will always be Nutley.

PLAYING HOUSE

*I*t wasn't easy growing up in Nutley in the early fifties. None of the girls on our block knew jack shit about playing house. All it meant to them was moving a few sticks of factory-made miniature furniture around beaverboard dollhouses with no back walls, or taking turns being the mommy and daddy.

The one person in the neighborhood who had even a smidgen of sense about how this classic childhood pastime should be played was Dale Davenport, a pale adolescent who lived two doors away. Dale shaved his underarms and legs and painted his toenails. This was fine with me because, though several years older, he seemed perfectly content to stay at home while I pursued business opportunities on the street and, as the breadwinner, confiscated younger children's snacks for our dinner table. With me and Dale, there *were* no turns.

Our first playhouse was a set of bedsheets thrown over chairs in the Davenports' basement. While this early use of fabrics and tenting would later reappear in my summer parties, books, and videos, the Johnny Ray–signature bottom sheet irritated me, and Dale suffered accordingly. From there we moved to a lofty, airy treehouse vacated by Tommy Fallon, a cocky ten-year-old from the street behind ours, after an untimely fall caused Mrs. Fallon to ban him from playing in trees for the rest of his boyhood. But the third and best playhouse Dale and I had was an old, abandoned Mercedes near the railroad tracks, where we pretended to be Polish white trash with suburban WASP aspirations.

Before long, however, I discovered that it was possible to set up half a dozen playhouses in different parts of the neighborhood, with different kids for spouses and children, simultaneously. By this time I had also gained a following among other girls in school. One early fan was Judith McPartland, a dumpy girl who followed me around like a pug in heat and who would jump off the Nutley Bridge if I told her to. (Contrary to stories in the local papers and her attorney's claims, she wasn't that badly hurt.)

At any rate, this is how we played the game, and it is the only way to play it.

The strongest child in the group gets to be head of the household. This child leaves for a while, pretending to go off to work. When she returns, the playhouse must be absolutely in order, with fresh picked dandelions in a jelly jar and candy for food on the table. If these things are not done, the offending spouse and other "family members" can be spanked with a hairbrush, switch (willow stings without breaking), or bare, sweating palm. From time to time—no one knows exactly when this is, it's just "time"—you raid other playhouses, taking useful household items, if any, and tying the occupants up using half-inch-thick, natural-fiber rope and kidnappers' knots. Sometimes the houses themselves are of value, in which case you evict the owners, move in, and renovate. Most of the time, however, they're inferior structures. It's fun to watch them burn.

By the next year I had abandoned playing house for a pyramid involving doll hair-care products. Dale would go on to become a senior executive at Time Warner, my former publisher (you would think by now he would have come out of the closet, but I've never heard anything, so perhaps not). Judith dropped out of school in the ninth grade to stalk Pat Boone. Today, from what I understand, she still enjoys playing house, though in Bellevue Hospital.

Me, I've managed to keep busy over the years (ha ha). But as is true of most experiences in childhood, playing house taught me lessons I would later apply when it came time to set up real house, with a real spouse, in real life: Always put the title in my name.

OUR LADY OF SUSPICIOUS CONCEPTION

elieve it or not, I owe part of my success to a few adults who spotted in me the seeds of genius and who proved somewhat useful as a result.

Most of all I remember two teachers at Our Lady of Suspicious Conception, the Catholic grammar school I attended as a girl. These were Sisters of Little Mercy, a Polish-Italian order of dense but volatile women devoted to the veneration of a fifth-century pizza bearing an uncanny resemblance to Saint Odo.

From my first-grade teacher, Sister Mary Pugnacious, I heard inspiring stories of girls who suffered for their beliefs; they would become models

of womanhood for me. There was Saint Theresa of the
Holy Gums, who took a rock and smashed in her baby
teeth in order to be able to receive First Communion.
And there was Saint Lucy of the Profusely Bleeding
Heart who, when lusted after by a lewd king, clutched
her blossoming breasts in both hands and ripped them
from her chest in order to deflate his desire.

Later, in the sixth grade, Sister Angela Bellicose
instilled a love of discipline that would stand me in
good stead as a businesswoman. When I was struggling
to get my catering career off the ground, or launch my
magazine, or become a fixture on network television, I
instinctively knew how to draw forth the best
performances from my employees: I did what Sister
Angela would do, and slapped them silly like
schoolchildren in detention!

It's not surprising, then, that in my twelfth year I
received a calling to become a nun myself. In
preparation, I dressed up as a Sister of Little Mercy on
Halloween and won the role of Mary in the Christmas
play (after Eileen Toomey had an accident on the
playground the day before the performance, breaking
both her arms and legs). More and more, I found
myself daydreaming about coming back to teach at

Suspicious Conception. I pictured myself walking slowly up and down the aisles, the dry rustling of my floor-length black habit raising hairs on the back of students' necks. Without warning I would come down hard with my metal ruler on the laps of boys caught staring at girls' patent-leather shoes in an attempt to see up their skirts.

My vocation, you see, was nothing less than the salvation of my classmates' souls. These I depicted by drawing oval-shaped outlines on the blackboard. With Sister Angela's encouragement, I filled in each "soul" with the side of the stick of chalk, representing "sin." This was not "original sin," I explained to the visibly nervous class, but new sins of lust and the flesh.

Today I sometimes find myself wondering how things would have turned out had I answered the calling. Certainly I would have been Mother Superior of the order by now. Or perhaps the first female Jesuit, in charge of the twenty-first-century Inquisition. Or Pope Martha.

Come to think of it, there's still time.

HOME EC

*I*n the same way that there were teachers who inspired me, and nurtured my talents, and made a difference in my life when I was young, there were many more employees of the lower educational system who wanted to see me fail. Mrs. Cornflower, who taught home ec my junior year of high school, was such a teacher.

They say the student who doesn't surpass her teacher fails her teacher, but this is an axiom to which Cornflower obviously didn't subscribe. From the first day of class, she seemed to take an instant dislike to me—why, I still have no idea. I remember finding my assigned seat at an island work station by the windows and starting to unload supplies from my rucksack: personal measuring cups, collection of tin gelatin and mousse molds, revolving cake stand, loins of pork and veal, a live guinea hen, a head of endive, set of tempered and balanced knives and skewers, etc. Suddenly, her considerable shadow fell across the countertop.

"What do you think you're doing?" Cornflower demanded.

"Making preparations for an A-plus," I answered confidently.

"Well, you'll have to do a lot *less* than this to get an A from me, Miss Preparation H," she said to her own amusement and to the titters of the other girls in class, stupid little twats. "You'll use the utensils and ingredients I hand out, just like everyone else. Do I make myself clear?"

"Yes, you're quite transparent, Mrs. Cornholer," I replied. No one laughed but me.

And so it went all year long, thrusting and parrying in this manner until her final lunge, near the end of the school year, when she accused me of cheating on the flan portion of the final exam. *Me!*

To this day I don't know what possessed the

woman to behave the way she did. Perhaps she felt
threatened by my natural facility in the kitchen. (It
wasn't the first time; it wouldn't be the last.)
Whatever the reason, I'll never know now. Sadly, Mrs.
Cornflower died shortly before the end of the term,
an apparent suicide. They found her in the big
industrial mixing bowl in the back of the classroom,
facedown in a week-old batch of hollandaise, with the
beaters still going at high speed.

Although all of us received A's for the term, I never
did learn what grade she intended to give me for the
course. Inexplicably, her gradebook was never found.

COLLECTING

My love affair with collectible objects began when I was very young and quite obsessed with lunch boxes. By the age of eleven, I had acquired the lunch boxes of all of my classmates save one; when he died suddenly at school one day from contaminated lunchmeat, his mother, in her grief, agreed to my low but sincere bid and my collection was complete!

Today, most people assume that my collecting is confined to domesticana, such as tin gelatin molds (currently on loan to the traveling Gelatin Museum exhibit), or hot-glue guns (the largest and most valuable collection in the world), or, well, houses. But

they're wrong. While it's true that I do possess
magnificent examples of almost every aspect of home
and gardening ware, my interests and passions know
no bounds, really.

Here are some of my favorite, though less well
known, collections:

- dustballs
- cat hairballs
- owl coughballs
- string cheese balls
- medieval dental instruments
- aged organ meats
- handcuffs
- antique tongue depressors
- classroom hygiene films from the fifties
- psychiatric patient restraints
- money
- Depression-era glass eyes

You may not want to collect the same objets as I.
Who would? They're none *left!* But seriously, should
you become interested in an area of collecting that is
undiscovered and underpriced, please drop me a line.
Be sure to include your address and the hours you
won't be home.

SENIOR PROM

*M*y date for the prom senior year was a shy junior named Stuart Stuart. I had always dated boys named Stuart (see "Becoming Me"), but Stuart Stuart's parents happened to own half of Nutley, for one thing, and the right half of Nutley, for another. What's more, he was an extremely tall Stuart, which meant his face wouldn't be competing with mine in prom photos.

Normally, Stuart Stuart wouldn't have been the kind of boy to ask a girl, any girl, to a prom. But we had a little talk in the hall one day between classes—technically, I was in the hall; he was in his locker—and in time he came to see things my way.

You probably think that I sew, bake, garden, and make shit for pleasure, that I came by all this knowledge and skill by design or out of boredom. Dumb fat twit! I learned to sew because I *had* to!

For weeks before the prom, while the rest of the town worked or slept, I was out scavenging fabric for my gown: swatches of sheets from neighbors' clotheslines; samples of panties and slips and tennis uniforms from the girls' locker room; a small square of white canvas from a convertible parked in a driveway on the other side of the tracks; gathered milkweed silk and light dog hair; and the white stripes from American flags.

Stuart's parents, Mr. and Mrs. Stuart, picked me up at seven-thirty on prom night in Mr. Stuart's Cadillac, a red convertible with a white roof. It was raining but the top was up so we were dry, at least in the backseat, though a small, perfect square of rain fell on Mrs. Stuart's head in the front. I had them drop us off directly in front of the Nutley High gym. I ran in ahead of Stuart, already knowing in my dry bones that the night belonged to me.

Needless to say, I was crowned prom queen a few hours later, and the dress I'd made from scratch won

Most Original Gown, putting other girls' gowns to shame (which, in the end, was the whole point). I know raw talent had much to do with my victories, but I also believe that determination and, yes, destiny played significant roles. More valuably, this would serve as a lesson for the rest of my life: When you really, *really* want something, others see it in your eyes and they get the hell out of your way.

FRUITCAKES

*F*ruitcake is one of my most popular
desserts, and gay men are some of
my biggest fans. The two go together like fruit and,
well, fruitflies. This might seem like an extraordinary
coincidence, but not when you look closely at the
"ingredients." The fruits called for in my recipe are
standard, orchard-variety cherries, plums, lemons,
oranges, and kiwis. Similarly, the fruitcakes I seem to
attract, and in huge numbers, are classic homos—
colorful and tasteful. I'm well aware that I have a
reputation for being insensitive to other people's
feelings. Yet whenever a fan or friend who happens to

be a fruit flies in for a visit, I make sure to serve him a slice of my fruitcake. After all, it is the little gestures in life that let others know how much you care.

MODELING

$\mathcal{A}$fter being discovered on my college campus by New York's hottest photographer, it didn't take long for the magazine world to realize it had found the "new face" everyone had been looking for. This was no revelation to me, frankly. I always knew I was blessed with stunning good looks. Where they came from is a question for the ages, but if you've ever seen my mother guest-cooking on my television show, it's more than obvious she played a minimum part, genetically speaking. This leads me to believe that at a very early age I simply willed my cells, on a molecular level, to serve as productive little beauty factories, each striving and recombining to become the best cell it could be. And when they all worked together, with my mind as the cosmetic architect, voilà!

In those days, models went on "go-sees"—half-assed auditions where one would show up at a photographer's studio or magazine office to do a little dog-and-pony show. This involved prancing around, showing off your portfolio, your runway walk, and your ass. If there was a heterosexual anywhere in sight, it was critical to make serious eye contact with the tacit promise that if the job was yours, you were his.

Of course, by the time you'd shot the actual assignment, it would be a cold day in hell before you remembered ever meeting the letch in the first place.

During these wasted hours sitting around with a bunch of airhead mannequins waiting for a chance to pose for a Summer's Eve douche spot, I honed my tactical skills. It's amazing what an innocently spilled cup of blazing-hot coffee will do to a competitor's photos, not to mention the legs beneath them. Even a casual aside, noting that a particular girl had the hots for a man who was famous for crab farming (if you know what I mean), could work wonders. Success was simply a matter of winnowing down the field until it was me and the chubette from Saltlick, Arkansas. Who would you have cast?

BECOMING ME

Fans have always assumed I was born Martha Stuart, so perfectly does it go with my looks and image. But believe it or not, I thought up the name for myself when I was a young girl. Even then I knew who I was, or at least, who I would become. All I needed was to find a young man with the appropriate last name.

When the time was right, I began looking in earnest for acceptable Stuart men: Ivy League education, parents with money, passive by nature, *more or less* heterosexual. It didn't take me long. Here's an entry from the diary I kept in college:

*Getting ready to go to a mixer. Have a feeling
tonite's the nite I'll meet "him." Early this
morning, while still dark, broke into the Student
Activities Council office at Princeton & checked
the sign-up sheet. (Don't worry: ripped the phone
out so there'd be no record of my call earlier in
the day to ask when the office closed.) Sure
enough, three undergrads and one grad student
named Stuart signed up for the mixer—including
a Stuart Stuart! Am so excited! Wearing
handmade chiffon undergarments from a pattern I
found in* Redbook *and enough Eau d'Bidet to
seduce an alley cat. Wish me luck. Love ya.*

How young and naive I was then. Luck had
nothing to do with it.

LOVE LIFE

here seems to be endless speculation in
the media about my love life. I've even
been called the *L* word, which is ridiculous. Why
would I be interested in women? They're useless.
They can't lift heavy objects, they spend inordinate
amounts of time talking, and when they're not
empathizing with another woman, they're having
babies. Not that there's anything wrong with babies. I
think I even have a daughter, if I'm not mistaken. (If
in fact I do, and if I forgot about her, I want to offer
her a formal apology here and now. I was busy, okay?)

But I've known love. I know the feeling I get when
the chickens' eggs come out the color of Necco

wafers, and in exactly the right order, or when the dogs relieve themselves in attractive patterns on the lawn. And I felt love flow inside me when I rang the bell at the New York Stock Exchange the morning of my IPO and saw all the little tent poles pop up among the brokers ready to trade me.

I know love. I know me.

ANALYSIS

*T*here comes a point in every woman's life when she must question her fundamental beliefs and values, confront her deepest doubts and fears, and come to terms with her limitations and failures, if she is to change and grow. Personally, I have no doubts, fears, limitations, failures, or values. But I once had an issue for a short while, and here is how I resolved it.

My period of soul searching luckily coincided with an opportunity to enter professional analysis. To tell you the truth, I'd never put much faith in therapy until then, believing that the time and effort it required could be much better spent telling other people how to live, then charging them up the wazoo for the advice.

This, however, was just too good an opportunity to pass up. It also happened to be mandatory, the result of a coincidence in which one of my cars and one of my neighbors' gardeners attempted to occupy the same space at the same time. The official charges filed against me were operating a battery-powered aide while driving, vehicular harassment, misuse of a Range Rover, excessive speed in a lawn zone, failure to brake for an illegal immigrant, and attempted hit-and-back-up-then-hit-again-runover-and-finally-just-run. Of course, as anyone who knows me knows, my real "crime" was possession of class, taste, and superiority.

A U.S. district court judge on Long Island appointed Dr. Susan Ripschitz, a therapist and anger-management specialist, to evaluate me, following which she would recommend either a program of treatment or incarceration. I arrived at her Southampton home office on a Monday morning, bearing a gift of an herbal douche I'd concocted that morning in my Hamilton Beach blender using catnip from the garden.

"So," she began, seated in a Naugahyde chair and

wearing a knockoff Donna Karan blouse. "Why don't you tell me in your own words why you're here."

"Why are *you* here?" I countered wittily.

"I'm here to help you, if you'll let me," she said in a calm, patient voice meant to be reassuring but kindling in me a strong desire to wrap my hands around her neck and twist her head off like a rooster before it becomes coq au vin.

Instead, I slowly scanned the office and outer hallway and rooms. "How can you expect to help me," I said, "when you obviously can't even take care of your own house?"

Ripschitz's smile faded like last week's petunias. "How exactly do you mean?" she inquired.

"Susan, Susan, Susan," I said, smiling and shaking my blond head. "You lazy, lazy bitch. For starters, you've used cheap, tacky, imitation-wood frames to frame your degrees and certificates when, for no money at all, you could have made real wood frames from that maple tree in your backyard. We're ambivalent about our accomplishments, aren't we?"

Almost imperceptibly, Ripschitz nodded.

"Also, you've set out a glass candy bowl of red Chuckles in a green-dominated room," I noted.

"Unless you celebrate Christmas in June, these colors should never be mixed."

The doctor looked depressed.

"And why," I said, "have you covered every sofa and armchair in your living room in plastic slipcovers?" (I'd peaked in the downstairs windows before my appointment!) "If you care more about upholstery than your guests' comfort, use a spot remover made of four parts Madeira vinegar to one part horse sweat." (If there's one kind of people I can't stand, it's anal relatives.)

For a long moment, Ripschitz stared at the unstenciled floor. Then her chin buckled and her lips quivered. "I can't do it all," she sobbed. "I just *can't.*"

I came around behind her to comfort her. In the process, I just happened to glance at a note she'd made on the legal pad on her desk. "Fits early psychological profile of Mussolini," it read. I thought, This woman isn't so bad after all!

"I know you can't," I said, putting my hands on her shoulders. "*That* is why I'm here."

Forty-five minutes later, when I left the office, I'd signed her up for a three-year subscription to my magazine and a gilding workshop at my home, got the

contract to cater the annual Anger Management
Dinner Dance at the Country Club of Naugatuck,
plus her evaluation of me, which reads as follows:
"I have evaluated Martha Stuart (case #56718,
Himenez v. Stuart), per the instructions of the U.S.
District Court of East Hampton, New York.

*Ms. Stuart submitted to the Rorschach, the
Borschtbowl, and the Ripschitz Flip-Out Response tests.
As a result, it is my conclusion that Ms. Stuart is a
rational, highly intelligent, and compassionate
individual, a caring wife and mother, and the best cook,
caterer, gardener, and housekeeper in the country. It is my
strong recommendation that all charges against her be
dropped and, furthermore, that the plaintiff, Mañuel
Himenez, be immediately referred to me for treatment of
grandiosity, paranoia, and chronic prevarification.*

So ended my first and last experience with
analysis. As a result, I must confess I've become a true
believer in therapy: I truly believe Dr. Ripschitz got a
lot out of our little session together.

POSEURS

*I*n case you didn't notice, anyone who can burn water has their own cable show these days. I am astounded by the arrogance of these poseurs who call themselves chefs. Take the mother of them all, Julia Child. Doesn't she think it's about time to hang up the toque before she hurts herself? Does anyone even care about friggin' consummé anymore? And while we're at it, what's she doing spreading a pound and a half of butter on that slice of toast? By now her heart must be the size of a family loaf of Silvercup White!

Then there's Mr. France, Jacques Pepin. I don't know about you, but if I hear one more word in

Frenglish spoken with a lithp, I'm going to kill my personal assistant. Which brings us to Mr. Italy, Mario Batali. His show is called *Mario Eats Italy*, when it should be *Mario* Ate *Italy*. Are you kidding? This guy is the greatest advocate for extra-virgin olive oil since Vito Corleone! Not to mention that wardrobe: too-long cargo shorts tucked up under that mammoth paunch and hanging over Day-Glo orange rubber clogs. Coco Chanel must be spinning like a dreidel in her grave.

I've saved the greatest pretender for last. A man who singlehandedly blasted the culinary arts back to Illinois in the fifties. You know who I mean—Mr. Bam, Emeril Lagasse. With the cooking skills of a drunken parolee grillman on work-release from Pelican Bay Penitentiary, Lagasse is the black hole of food preparation.

But at the end of the day, as I settle into my 4,000-thread-count, bee's-wing sheets for seven minutes of quality REM sleep, I rest soundly knowing that if it weren't for me, I wouldn't be here.

$\mathcal{M}$y paternal ancestors, photographed in their native Noland (now northern Poland), where they were renowned as vole hunters and fecephiles. Forced to flee after enactment of the Personal Hygiene Laws, they're shown here en route to New Jersey, where they would find themselves culturally and intellectually at home.

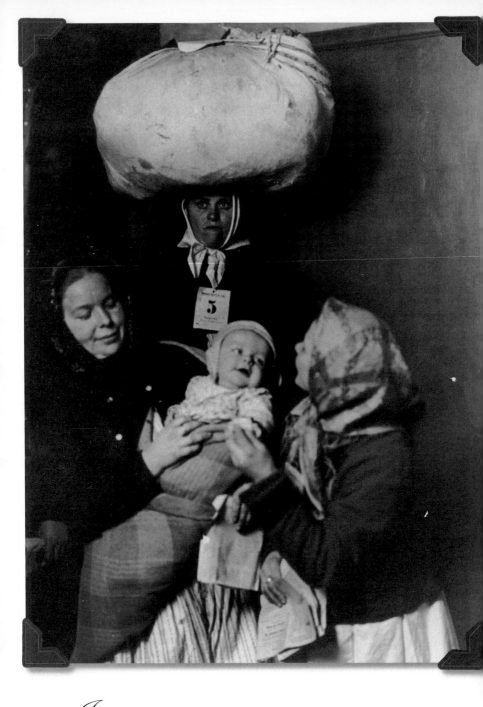

$\mathcal{I}$ was surrounded by strong female role models early in life, and named after my great aunt, Martha the Often Leborked, number 5 in this photograph. Here, she has caught, trussed, and bundled a small man for the Monday night Sadie Hawkins dance in her village.

*A*nother successful operation: Dr. Martha, age six, with patient Pooh Bear following an emergency nose job, lip reduction, jaw realignment, lobotomy, rectalectomy, gender bypass, and partial double amputation. Sooo cute.

$\mathcal{A}$ traditional Mother's Day bake-off with Mom, which my father always judged. I don't believe she ever won.

$\mathcal{H}$ouseguests at Turkey Hill love to pitch in with gardening and seasonal decorating, sometimes even paying for the privilege, as did this guest.

The buildings and grounds at Turkey Hill compound in Connecticut.

Parent's Guest
Quarters

Guilding
Studio

Arugula Salad Garden

Leather
Shop

Stallion Patch

...atoir

Maison
de
mierde

Geotherma...
Cappuccin...
Steam Val...

...cargot Pond

Control
Central

Mined-Croquet
Lawn

Co...

Main Driveway

$\mathscr{I}$ began collecting glue guns in early adolescence, when the steady flow of hot adhesive aroused my interest. Shown here is part of an exhibit of my guns currently at the Musée du Mucilage in Paris. Included are a rare Hammimoto Hummingbird from the 1930s, far left, and next to it, a Bindorff Magnum .44 once owned by Eva Braun.

*D*iscipline is an underrated virtue in American society today, but for me it has been the key to success in business and in life. Here I conduct a one-on-one discipline workshop with a greenhouse worker at one of my houses. Now he appreciates the deep meaning and joy of this virtue too.

𝓜other chose one of the busiest days of my calendar year—Mother's Day—for an unannounced visit. Fortunately, I'd just finished designing this Eldercare Confinement Arbor, which allows baby boomers the freedom to garden while enjoying the company of elderly parents. ($1,436.55 at Kmartha).

$\mathcal{I}$'m always testing new products, like this potential entry in the premium beer market, Martha Stewedski Brewski. You know me: I won't quit until the taste is perfect. Perhaps a teensy bit more alcohol.

$\mathcal{T}$ag, yard, and garage sales have always been an important part of my life. It is here that I've found most of the props for my magazine and shows, as well as furnishings for my houses and gifts for my family and friends. One way or another, I never fail to leave with what I've come for. Never.

$\mathcal{M}$y East Hampton home is usually the first stop for His Holiness when touring North America. It's Polish, it's spotless, and it's chaste, goddamnit!

*I*n what has become a tradition whenever we're together, John Paul and I engage in some friendly water-to-wine competition. He has never won.

 $\mathscr{E}$ ven the pope needs to get things off his chest from time to time. He knows his secrets will be safe with me, even that incident involving the eunuchs and the . . . Whoops.

$\mathcal{A}$lthough my daughter didn't want a Martha Stuart–style reception, I managed to play a central role in her marriage—and her life—anyway (heh heh).

MARRIAGE

I'll never forget my wedding. Although my parents didn't have the money for the kind of reception I deserved, I did amazing things with the materials on hand. Here is the menu from that special day:

- A&P ginger ale, decanted and poured into Dom Pérignon bottles retrieved from the Dumpster behind Le Cirque
- Aged cheeses (Cheez Whiz white & gold, in spray cans with expired dates), on used Pepperidge Farm crackers
- Fresh wild salad greens (lawn cuttings from the maintenance shed in Central Park)

- Grilled Atlantic (East River, actually) sea trout (carp, actually)
- Roast Squab au Square du Temps
- Légumes de Martha (Birds Eye frozen green beans in undiluted Campbell's mushroom soup topped with canned Durkey fried onion rings)
- Wedding pound cake with prefab, basket-weave icing

Once the last of the guests were shown the door, I went around to all of the tables and gathered up the leftovers. When I re-served them at another catering job two weeks later, some of the same guests were able to enjoy them all over again! (Entertaining tip #1348: cut partially eaten food at the bite marks, brown exposed edges with acetylene torch, serve as new!)

To preserve the memory of that most romantic of occasions, I've kept the wedding cake all these years in the refrigerated pastry safe in the basement of my Connecticut home. Someday, when I'm finally over the pain of that miserable reception, I'm going to cut the cake. And when I do, slices of that sucker will fetch an freakin' fortune on eBay!

WALL STREET

*A*s it is for most newlyweds, money was tight those first few years of marriage. Tighter than I thought it would be, actually. Tighter than I'd been led to believe, to tell you the truth. Tighter by far than had appeared in the original script for my home video *Martha Stuart Marries a Millioinaire.*

In the early '70s, I set out to conquer Wall Street with the same enthusiasm I would later bring to neutering pets, say, or stenciling my employees' bodies. I guess because I was a woman at a time when very few women worked on the Street, no record

exists today of my accomplishments. But trust me
when I say I was fabulously successful.

I had many close friends in Manhattan by this
point, and naturally I thought of them first whenever
a particularly hot stock appeared on my radar screen.
One of my first and hottest picks was Lovitz or
Leavitz, the legendary high-end home furnishings
company that manufactured Lazy Suzannes, among
other classic pieces. But there were many others:
DeLorean Motor Company, Saul Steinberg's Reliance
Insurance Company, Equity Funding, the Bowmar
Instrument Corp., Pet Rocks Ltd., *ImClone*. The list
went on and on and on.

This will come as a complete surprise to readers,
but the stock I most believed in at the time—and the
only one I thought had a future—was mine. And my
real motive in gaining access to the New York Stock
Exchange was to scout the floor for a party I
envisioned myself hosting one day as uniformed
employees passed endless trays of canapés and I rang
open the trading day, setting off a feeding frenzy for
shares of Martha Stuart Inc.

It was a wacky dream, I know, but it sustained me.

Regrettably, however, life sometimes disappoints. Not me, but my former friends. Although I did remarkably well, my stock picks for them weren't quite as profitable. They claimed they had preexisting agreements with me to sell if their stocks fell below a certain price per share. But I have no recollection of this and no written agreements have ever been found. In fact, all of my clients' records disappeared during the investigation, as did my assistant, who was preparing to testify against me. To this day, I feel the loss deeply. Those records were in perfect order.

Whatever. They lost and I didn't. They moved back in with their parents; I moved on. They're still bitter; I'm happy. I'm writing my autobiography; they're not. I . . .

Oh well, you get the picture. Let's move on to the next chapter.

TURKEY HILL

*L*ike Thomas Jefferson's Monticello or the Kennedy compound in Hyannisport, Turkey Hill epitomizes American accomplishment, status, and power. Unlike the tacky Virginia tourist attraction or that paparazzi pit in Massachusetts, however, my Connecticut home is a working estate—things get done here, for God's sake—not to mention a freaking moola machine!

In the late sixties, while other attractive young couples were leaving suburban homes for communes in California, my new husband and I traded apartment life in New York City for an old farmhouse on Turkey Hill Road in Westport. (I chose the town because of

its WASPy, artsy reputation, and because my
reputation hadn't yet spread there from Nutley or
Manhattan. It was my idea to name the property
"Turkey Hill.")

Some of my most cherished memories of marriage
and family life reside here.

What I love most about the place is that I
accomplished this all by myself.

In recent years, Turkey Hill has become a mecca
for women the world over who travel thousands of
miles, some on their knees, for a glimpse of the house,
gardens, and outbuildings (see map in center photo
album) from behind the guard towers and 1,200-volt,
double–concertina wire fence.

Neighbors accuse me of profiting from these
ninnies, but look what they get for the price of
admission (*admission* may be too strong a word in this
context; perhaps *price of observation* would be a more
accurate phrase): For a measly Jackson, visitors get
their choice of a deadheaded flower or a pellet of
poulet droppings, packaged in an attractive plastic
baggie, plus an ink stamp of my face on their hands so
they won't be hauled off by members of my security
force.

Turkey Hill

Of greatest attraction for these women, of course,
is the chance to glimpse me. (I can't tell you how
much hope this arouses in these pathetic creatures'
hearts, because have no idea why they're here.) There
isn't a particularly *good* chance of seeing me—it hasn't
happened *yet*—but the point is, it *could* happen, I
suppose.

The one catch is that I don't actually live in the
house at Turkey Hill, and haven't for many years.
Thanks to my neighbors, home for me is a concrete
bunker beneath the radiccio garden on the property,
some fifty feet from the main house. I know that this
bombshell is going to cause great concern among my
fans. But frankly, the bunker suits my personality, is
easy to maintain, and provides the level of security
I've always longed for. Don't worry, I'm very
comfortable here. It's stocked with a year's supply of
TV dinners (has anyone tried the Salisbury steak
lately? Yumm), fifty-five-gallon drums of Häagen-
Dazs, and enough Ring Dings to circle Uranus.

Yet these are small comforts indeed for what I've
endured at the hands of neighbors and townspeople. I
snapped my fingers and there were lights, action,
illusion! Twenty-four/seven, there were cable trucks,

helicopters, makeup people, camera crews, key grips, and best boys. I put Turkey Hill Road and Westport, Connecticut, on the friggin' map! And how have I been repaid? With lawsuits. With cease-and-desist orders nailed to my door. With magazines parodying my every bowel movement (see "Imitation, Irritation, Litigation, Colonic Irrigation").

For a brief period, I seriously considered moving away. But no. I think I'll stay. In fact, I'm never leaving Turkey Hill. They're going to have to pry the hot-glue gun from my cold, dead fingers. Why, you might ask? Because I *do* wish me on my worst enemy.

For there could be no sweeter revenge than having me for a neighbor.

IMITATION, IRRITATION, LITIGATION, COLONIC IRRIGATION

*I*n the fall of 1993, following the phenomenal success of *Martha Stuart Living*, a couple of middle-aged, middle-class morons published a parody of my magazine entitled, *Is Martha Stuart Living?* Not sufficiently amused, Connor and Downey, the literary wankers in question, followed this with a second spoof: *Martha Stuart's Better Than You at Entertaining.*

Now I have as good a sense of humor as anybody, but the way these two Irish idiots portray me in their scurrilous, sacrilegious rags amounts to character assassination. They show me throwing a police wrist-lock on a fellow tag-sale shopper in order to procure a

MARTHA, REALLY AND CRUELLY

vase she found and I wanted (not the way it really happened); murdering a neighbor's sheep to make natural lamb condoms (its death was ruled an accident); backing over pet chicks in the driveway to obtain templates for a chick-motif stencil (I can explain this); presenting dinner guests with a check for appetizers and entrées (it was a very expensive dinner!).

What kind of heartless harps would write things like this? What, do they sit around in their underwear all day, drinking Guinness and thinking up cruel, labor-intensive, time-consuming, over-the-top projects for their "Martha" to perform?

Judging from taped phone conversations and surveillance photos, Connor appears to be the smaller and stupider of the two—a half-pint half-wit who is obviously threatened by my size and success. When asked by one interviewer why they chose to parody me, he replied, "Imitation is the sincerest form of flatulence." I have a sneaking suspicion he wasn't being flattering.

As the micks without dicks commanded more and more media attention, and as their parodies climbed the best-seller list, I began experiencing a deep, inner irritation, the likes of which I'd never known. A good deal of this, no doubt, was brought on by my frustration at not being able to sue their asses: It seems that a little-known constitutional loophole—something called "First Amendment rights"(?)—prevented my lawyers from litigating.

Worse, fans of mine who were given the books as jokes or as insults frequently mistook them for the real thing, writing to tell me how much they enjoyed the obscene recipes and cruel instructions.

Ultimately, the Mr. Potato Heads caused me so much distress that I developed creative blockage and required colonic irrigation—not once but over and over, in and out, up and down, again and again and again and again and again. (Since this is a relatively expensive procedure, I saved money by having my plumber perform it using a simple tool from his toolbox.)

Now, however, with the publication of *Martha Stuart's Excruciatingly Perfect Weddings* several years ago, the buffoons' self-titled Martha Parody trilogy is complete. At last, I can return to the life of privacy I so crave.

Yet all the while, throughout the nearly decade-long ordeal at the hands of those potato pickers, one aspect of the parodies continues to trouble and elude me: What, I'd like to know, is *so freaking funny?*

Is it *funny* that I'm the enormous butt of their asinine jokes? Is it *funny* that I'm portrayed as some kind of anal-compulsive mental case with a Hitlerian power complex (also see chapter entitled "Analysis")? Is it a scream, a howl, a fucking hoot to see me make water, make dirt, glue dead things to other things, use a corpse as a dinner-table centerpiece?

But then it isn't just these two micks who have been laughing, is it? Someone had to *buy* the parodies, didn't they? In fact, more than a million of you, as in turns out, have supported Connor and Downey at my expense.

No, go ahead, have yourselves a good laugh. As you read this, my corporate security force is scouring secret publishing records for those years. Soon, I'll have the names and addresses of every man, woman, and child who ever bought or even looked at the parodies. And when I do, I'm going to hunt you down like truffles buried under the trunks of trees routed out by snarling, drooling, grunting, gluttonous wild pigs!

Then we'll see who's having the big yucks!

KMARTHA

K

K

*I*n 1986, I embarked upon one of the most successful business relationships in retailing history when Kmart approached me to develop a line of my products for their stores.

At the time, many wondered if the Gruyère had slipped off my Ritz. Martha Stuart getting involved with Kmart was like me doing the dirty deed with Joey Buttafuoco, rolling around in 10-40 oil on his filthy garage floor while he raced my engine and shifted my gears, taking me higher and higher like some hydraulic lift gone berserk oh hotdamn you Joey you steaming man-plate of tumescent ziti!

If I had my reasons for teaming up with the chain,

no one knew them. For once in my life I held my tongue.

The first product for the Martha Kmart line was a backyard composter for dead pets and guests retailing for $499.98. Within three months, the line had expanded to include exorbitantly priced versions of such basic household items as Martha-brand mucilage spreaders, home colonoscopy kits, Metamucil spoons, tabletop crumb blowers and vacuums, julienne pocketknives, grilled-cheese irons, home stun guns, and much, much more.

In the early years of the new millennium, with the economy slowing and competitor chains gaining market share, I jacked my prices higher still. Before long, buckling under the weight of a binding agreement that guaranteed me profits regardless of sales, Kmart declared bankruptcy. (Reports that I dumped my shares in the company the day before the filing were greatly exaggerated.)

Publicly, I voiced concern while vowing to support the company. Privately, I rubbed my hands in glee. My plan was working perfectly!

As you've turned the pages of this book, my attorneys and mergers and acquisitions people have been in secret session with Kmart directors at company headquarters in Troy, Michigan (Troy!). In exchange for a few minor concessions, I've agreed to lower prices for my products and rescind the binding profit agreement.

Soon, Kmart will emerge from Chapter 11 with me as chief executive officer and the company with a brand new name and identity! "Clean up in the former executive aisle!"

FAVORITE
RECIPES

People ask me all the time what my favorite recipes are. Here, I'm more than happy to share them with my fans and readers, to whom I owe so much.*

Martha's Bug Juice

Developed at sleep-away camp when I was ten, and sold first to cabin-mates at a discounted price and later to counselors, this recipe calls for nothing more than two mason jars of lightning bugs; ten pounds white sugar; red dyes #17, 49, 50, 51, and 236; twenty gallons medium-brown pond water; and one gallon Polish vodka.

Tybr Rudski (smoldering roots and tuber casserole)
An Old World dish handed down from Dumbrowski
to Dumbrowski (see "Ancestors"). It consists of beets,
onions, yams, rutabagas, and other rhizomes missed
during harvest, buried in coals of used building
materials, drizzled with rainwater, and eaten warm but
still smoking.

Hand-Mown Lawn and Meadow Salad
Surprisingly inexpensive, this wonderful salad can be
gathered just before dinner is to be served. Combine
marigold deadheads, two handfuls of mulch, one cup
peat moss, twelve dozen dandelions, and three cups
wild birdseed; season with lawn capers (rabbit or deer
droppings) to taste.

Smoked Woodchuck Appetizer
Sliced loin of woodchuck or hedgehog, marinated in
WD-40, and cooked over Martha's Briquettes that
have been dumped down its burrow and lit with a
flamethrower. Actually, in a pinch, any vermin will do.

Trussed Rump Roast

Basically just any huge hunk of cow cheek fist-infused with a pound of butter, severally bound with rope or chain, and roasted at 175 degrees for nine days.

Truman Compote

Seasonal East Hampton fruits lubricated in their own juices and glazed with alcohol.

Calamari Gelato

On family day trips to the Jersey shore, my mother would instruct us children to bring her whatever tentacles we would find lying on the beach and she would whip them into this wonderfully cooling summer dessert.

(*NB: If you use or attempt to use any of the aforementioned recipes or any portion thereof for any reason whatsoever without express written consent *and* prepaid user fee, members of my Royalty Collection and Enforcement staff will hunt you down and bring me back the small but nonetheless satisfying portion of your still warm and quivering sweetbreads. MS)

DATING
AGAIN

ne of the hardest things I've ever had to do was to begin dating again following my divorce. For one thing, my only romantic partner up until this point had been my ex-husband. For another, I had always been the one to ask him out. And for another, though this has never before been made public, he had lost a good deal of his manhood in a pruning accident in the latter stages of our marriage.

I knew men still found me attractive; on more than occasion, I'd caught the landscapers on my Hamptons estate collectively staring at my derriere and grunting appreciatively. All the same, I felt like a

schoolgirl again when Charlie Rose asked me out
during a station break on his televised talk show.

What's the kindest way to put this? Charlie's not
the long-stemmed variety, if you know what I mean.
Nor was Mort Zuckerman, the diminutive publisher
and real estate baron. I think "diminutive" sizes up the
problem rather concisely.

Still, it was nice to step out on the town with a
near peer, putting to rest certain rumors about my
preferences, and a sufficient warmup for my Big Date.

I've always thought John McLaughlin, the business
talk show host, was hot. There's something about
older men who wear suspenders to keep their suit
pants hoisted above their waists that just preheats my
oven! Naturally, I said yes, yes, *yes* when he asked me
out during a taping of the show.

Over the next two months, we saw each other two
or three times a week. A typical date went something
like this: After a quiet dinner together, we'd go back
to his place and dress up like a priest and nun
(apparently John did his homework; few others know
this, but my collection of nun habits is second only to
New York Cardinal Edward Egan's!). Then we'd chase
each other around his apartment. When I caught him,

I would force his confession and mete out the proper penance. Often this would involve spanking (his idea) but, increasingly, an involuntary colonic purge (mine).

Perhaps I should have gone easier on him. Or harder. Perhaps I should have let him get away a few times, or chase me. Whatever the reason, we parted amicably and remain good friends.

In other words, I'm currently available and am especially interested in meeting litigators, government investigators, or SEC employees (level 14 and above only). Call me.

I'M CLONIC

Near the end of 2001, the empire I had worked so hard to build was shaken to its foundations by a scandal of unimaginable unpleasantness. Many of you are no doubt familiar with the details of the insider-trading case against me from tabloids like the *Wall Street Journal* and the *New York Times*, but here, for the first time, is the true story behind the charges.

In the mid '90s, Peter Bacanovic, a friend of my daughter's from college and my broker at Merrill Lynch, recommended that I buy shares in ImClone, a company I believed at the time was interested in cloning me. ImClone's founder, Dr. Sam Waksal, had also been friendly with Alexis. Too friendly, as it turned out, going so far as to date her though he was more than twice her age (some men will do anything to get to me).

At any rate, for perhaps the only time in my life, I let my emotions overrule my intellect and bought several thousand shares of company stock.

In late December, Waksal learned that ImClone's application for a cancer drug was going to be rejected by the Food and Drug Administration. The day after Christmas, he and several relatives attempted to dump their shares before the bottom dropped out of the company's stock. In doing so, he not only beat me by a day in unloading *my* shares, he triggered full-blown investigations into the transaction by the SEC and Department of Justice, sending the value of stock in my company, OmnivoreMedia, plummeting.

I realize now that I committed a terrible error in judgment. If I could take back the entire episode, I gladly would. I violated a personal code I've tried to live by most of my adult life: *Never* invest in a company run by a short, bald man.

On looks alone, bald men cannot be trusted. Baldies (especially short, scrawny ones who wear baseball caps everywhere, as Dr. Sam did) are prone to cover-up. They deceive themselves with bad rugs and comb-overs while believing they're really deceiving others. They are constitutionally incapable of seeing themselves for what they are: bald. Besides, any doctor stupid enough to lose his hair certainly isn't smart enough to find a cure for cancer.

Other people, such as reporters and SEC investigators, have searched for incriminating evidence against me, but in vain. Under a preexisting agreement, my broker was to unload my shares of ImClone if Waksal's hairline fell below a certain point. On the morning of December 28, Peter received a call from Waksal's barber, saying the doctor's pate had advanced, like the desert, to below two inches on the sides and three inches in back, and he was considering a massive double comb-over to cover it up. Peter tried reaching me, first on my cell phone and then on the tin can strung between our offices (well, it's cheaper than cell phones and more reliable), but missed me. Given our unwritten understanding, however, he sold my entire portfolio of ImClone shares without needing to consult me.

Nearly two years have passed since the incident, but I'm still shaking with rage. Don't you see the pattern here? Not Male-Pattern Baldness, you idiots! The pattern of envy, resentment, revenge, and widespread hatred of me for my good fortune in life. The pattern of abuse of power and persecution of the innocent! But I'll be back. And when that happens, we'll see who's shaking.